LIVING IN HISTORY

A TUDOR SCHOOL

Peter Chrisp

Illustrations by Gerald Wood

Heinemann

CONTENTS

**Produced for Heinemann Children's Reference by
Roger Coote Publishing, Gissing's Farm
Fressingfield, Suffolk IP21 5SH**

Educational Consultant: Jane Shuter
Editorial Director: David Riley
Art Director: Cathy Tincknell
Production Controller: Lorraine Stebbing

First published in Great Britain in 1997 by
Heinemann Children's Reference
an imprint of Heinemann Educational Publishers
Halley Court, Jordan Hill, Oxford OX2 8EJ
a division of Reed Educational & Professional Publishing Ltd

MADRID ATHENS PRAGUE FLORENCE PORTSMOUTH NH
CHICAGO SAO PAULO SINGAPORE TOKYO MEXICO
MELBOURNE AUCKLAND IBADAN GABORONE
JOHANNESBURG KAMPALA NAIROBI

ISBN 0431 06824 0 (Hbk)   ISBN 0431 06825 9 (Pbk)

British Library Cataloguing in Publication Data
A catalogue record for this book is available from the British Library.

Printed and bound in Italy

TUDOR GRAMMAR SCHOOLS

In the 1590s, there were only two types of school in England. Petty schools taught very young boys and girls to read. Grammar schools taught Latin to boys aged between 6 and 15. Many books and official documents were written in Latin. You needed to know Latin to go to university, or to follow almost any career. Women did not go to university or have a career. So only boys went to a grammar school.

▲ A petty school was often in a cottage in the countryside, or in one room of a town house.

Grammar schools were paid for by private gifts of money. A rich nobleman or a group of merchants might decide that their town needed a grammar school. So they gave money to build the school, buy books and to pay the teachers' wages. People who weren't rich enough to pay to set up a school often left money for books or re-building in their will.

▼ The money needed to build a grammar school in a town often came from the wealthy merchants who lived there.

During the reign of Queen Elizabeth I (1558–1603), 136 new grammar schools were set up all over England. This book looks at what it was like to spend a day in one of them.

WHO'S WHO IN A TUDOR SCHOOL?

Most grammar schools had only two teachers, who lived in the school building. The master ran the school and taught the oldest boys. He was helped by a young assistant teacher called an usher, who taught simpler lessons to the younger pupils.

Both men wore long thick robes. A robe was a sign of respectability (like a modern business suit). Teachers, merchants, doctors and lawyers all wore robes. Robes also kept the teachers warm in the cold schoolroom.

▼ The boys in the school were between 6 and 15 years old. There was no school uniform, although many boys wore similar types of clothes.

▲ The master was aged between 40 and 50. He was a very stern man, and most of his pupils were terrified of him.

▶ The usher, who was in his early 20s, had been a monitor at the school. He hoped to become master of his own school one day.

▲ Before going to grammar school, most boys had already been to learn the alphabet in a petty school. These could be badly taught. There were always some boys who went on to grammar school unable to read.

The number of boys varied from school to school. A big London grammar school might have had 300 pupils, while a small country school often had just 20 boys. Most schools had between 50 and 100 boys.

The boys came from many backgrounds. They included the sons of nobles, merchants, lawyers, farmers, shopkeepers and craftworkers. Schools charged a fee, but it was often low, to give poorer children the chance to have an education. Some of the boys lived at home. Others, whose homes were too far away, lived in the school; they were called 'boarders'.

Two or three of the older boys were chosen to be monitors. They had to make sure that the other boys behaved themselves when the teachers were not there. They also taught the simplest lessons. They helped the youngest boys, or 'petties' (little ones), to learn the alphabet.

◀ This 15-year-old boy is a monitor.

▶ A kitchen-maid came to school every day to cook the meals and clean.

INSIDE THE SCHOOL

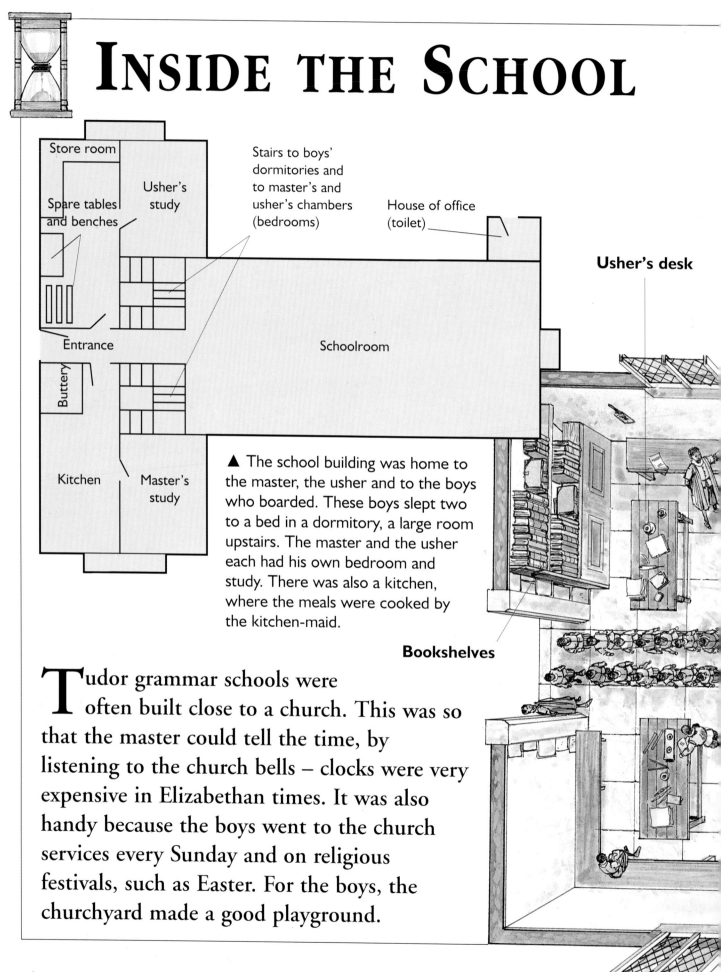

Store room

Spare tables and benches

Usher's study

Stairs to boys' dormitories and to master's and usher's chambers (bedrooms)

House of office (toilet)

Usher's desk

Entrance

Buttery

Schoolroom

Kitchen

Master's study

▲ The school building was home to the master, the usher and to the boys who boarded. These boys slept two to a bed in a dormitory, a large room upstairs. The master and the usher each had his own bedroom and study. There was also a kitchen, where the meals were cooked by the kitchen-maid.

Bookshelves

Tudor grammar schools were often built close to a church. This was so that the master could tell the time, by listening to the church bells – clocks were very expensive in Elizabethan times. It was also handy because the boys went to the church services every Sunday and on religious festivals, such as Easter. For the boys, the churchyard made a good playground.

▼ This is the schoolroom, where all the lessons were held. There are big windows to let in light, placed high up the walls. This was to stop the boys gazing out of the windows instead of paying attention to the teacher. There are chalkboards around the walls. The teachers wrote on these in chalk. Apart from the boards, the walls of the room were quite bare.

Many schools had a garden, for growing vegetables and herbs, and an orchard for fruit. There was a well for water and a 'house of office', a tiny outside toilet.

The master sat at one end of the schoolroom on a big chair. From this high seat, he could keep an eye on everything that went on. There were no desks. When the boys needed to write, they sat around the big tables, or rested their paper on their knees. There was only one fireplace – behind the master's chair – and in winter the room was bitterly cold.

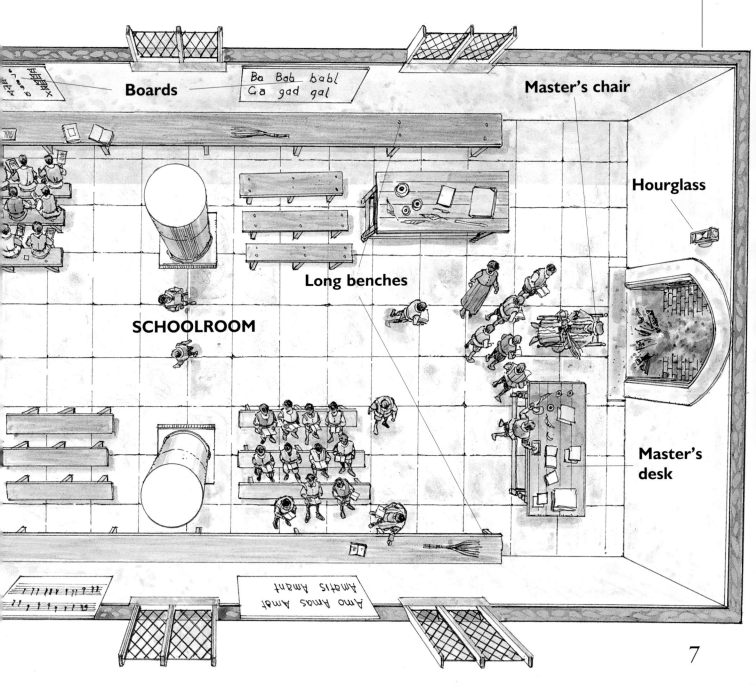

Boards

Ba Bab babl
Ga gad gal

Master's chair

Hourglass

Long benches

SCHOOLROOM

Master's desk

Amo Amas Amat
Amatis Amant

SCHOOL EQUIPMENT

The first piece of equipment used by every schoolboy was called a 'horn-book'. This was a flat piece of wood with a long handle. Fastened to it was a sheet of paper printed with letters and a prayer. The paper was covered with a very thin sheet of see-through horn to protect it. The youngest boys learned to read from these.

Once they could read, the boys were given two small textbooks. One was the *Primer,* or first reading book, a collection of prayers and questions and answers about religion. The other was William Lily's *Latin Grammar.* These books were cheaply made and had paper covers.

▲ A horn-book printed with the letters of the alphabet and the Lord's Prayer.

◄ Learning to read from a horn-book.

The school also owned some big expensive books with leather covers: the Bible, in Latin and in English; a Latin dictionary; and several books in Latin by ancient Roman writers.

◄ Large, leather-bound books like these were very expensive to buy and they were only used by the master, the usher and the oldest boys.

▶ The master and the usher sometimes used teaching aids such as this pictorial alphabet, flash cards and religious pictures to help boys learn to read or to explain difficult ideas.

Ink was made at the school, from a mixture of gum arabic (a sticky substance produced by trees), green vitriol (made from acid poured on old nails) and galls (small lumpy growths found on oak trees). Pens were cut from goose feathers. The most expensive equipment was paper, which was made abroad, in Italy and France.

A Methode.

ð	b	p	d	t
Sheares.	A Ball.	A Peare.	A Drum.	A Trumpet.
g	ʒ	v	d	2
A Grashopper.	A Ierkin.	A Vane.	The Sunne.	Zacheus.
k	c	f	ꝺ	s
A Key.	A Chaine.	A Filbert.	A Thimble.	A Squirrell.

¶ Here is to be noted, for that there is not in my remembrance the names of any thing which beginne with the soundes of d. or 2. I haue vsurped the article de, with the Sunne, for the best I could as yet thinke on: and the little man Zache, that climed in the wilde figge tree. Luke. xix.

¶ Now you may teach your Scholler, to remember the letters by the names of the portraitures, first the fiue vowels, forth and backe, which when he thinketh to know, you may doe the like with the rest, and when he hath so gone ouer all foorth and backe, then you may shew them vnto him downewardes and vpwarde, and when he thinketh to know the letter alone, you maye doe
B. ij.   well

The master carried a long bundle of birch twigs, which he used for beating the boys on their backsides. The amount of beating varied from school to school. Some masters only beat their boys for serious offences. But one master was said to beat his boys on cold mornings 'for no other purpose than to get himself warm.'

◀ Boys could be beaten for many offences, including fighting, gambling, stealing, swearing, telling lies, coming to school late, and talking in class.

THE DAY BEGINS

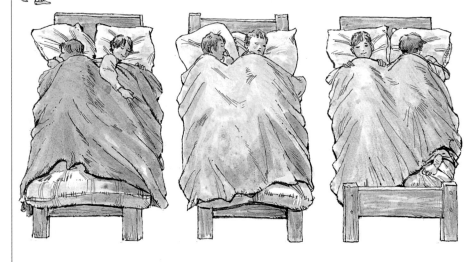

◀ The boys who stayed at the school slept upstairs in the dormitory. Two boys shared each bed.

▼ As soon as they got out of bed, the boys said their prayers.

The school day began early, before sunrise. At five in the morning, the boys who boarded had to get up. They said prayers, made their beds, got dressed and went downstairs.

Meanwhile, the rest of the boys were making their way along the streets from their homes. William Shakespeare, in his play *As You Like It* (written about 1599), describes one of these boys: 'And then the whining school-boy, with his satchel and shining morning face, creeping like a snail unwillingly to school.'

◀ When the boys went downstairs, they lined up outside to wash their hands and faces with cold water from the well.

The boy's satchel held paper, a goose-quill pen, a pen-knife, a pot of ink carved from horn, and wax candles, used to light the schoolroom on dark winter days. He had a 'shining morning face' because he had been scrubbing it. It was against the rules to come to school with a dirty face or hands.

▼ The master says prayers.

▲ Day boys might eat breakfast at home.

When the boys arrived at school, they found the usher waiting for them in the schoolroom. The boys took their hats off and greeted him. Then the master, who had just got out of his warm bed, came in. Everyone knelt and clasped their hands, while the master recited prayers in Latin or English.

▼ Breakfast at school.

After prayers, one of the monitors called out all the boys' names. He wrote down the names of those who had not appeared. Then he checked the boys' hands and faces for dirt. Dirty boys were sent outside to wash again.

Lessons began between six and seven o'clock, and continued for two hours. Then the boys had a light breakfast – usually bread and cheese, or pottage, with weak beer and, sometimes, an apple.

MORNING LESSONS

Imagine being in a room with five or six lessons all taking place at the same time. In one part of the schoolroom, the youngest boys were learning to read. They were taught by a monitor, who wrote short words on the boards. Across the room, the usher was teaching Latin grammar to a set of older boys. Meanwhile, the oldest boys of all were being questioned by the master. A Tudor schoolroom was a crowded, noisy place.

Once they had learned to read, the boys began memorising Latin words and learning the rules of Latin grammar. They read the rules in their textbooks and were tested on them by the usher. He repeated the same questions over and over until every boy knew the answers by heart.

▼ While the youngest boys (on the right) learn their ABC, older boys (left) learn Latin with the usher. The oldest boys are translating Latin into English for the master.

Amo Amas Amat

► Small, cheaply made Latin textbooks like this were used by all Tudor grammar-school boys.

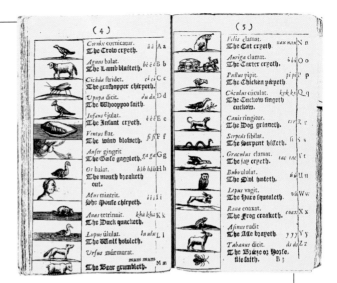

Older boys spent their time 'making Latins', translating short sentences from Latin into English, or from English into Latin. The sentences usually had a moral, such as 'There is nothing which God cannot do'. The oldest boys translated longer passages and wrote their own essays and poems in Latin.

All educated people were expected to know Latin. Across Europe, all the important books about science, law or religion were written in Latin. The language was described as 'the key to all knowledge'. It allowed writers from different countries to share their ideas with each other. If you wanted to become a lawyer, a churchman, a doctor or a civil servant, you had to know Latin.

DINNER TIME AND A WRITING LESSON

Morning lessons ended when the church bells rang out at eleven o'clock. There was now a two-hour break for the main meal of the day, dinner. The boys who lived nearby went home to eat. The rest ate in the schoolroom.

Pottage

The usual dinner was a bowl of pottage. This was a thick stew made with barley or oats, herbs and sometimes a little bacon or dried fish. In the cold schoolroom, the bowls of pottage gave the boys some welcome warmth.

▶ There was much more to writing than making letters. The boys also learned to cut pens from goose feathers with a 'pen-knife', the name we still use for a small pocket knife. Here you can see the stages in cutting a pen.

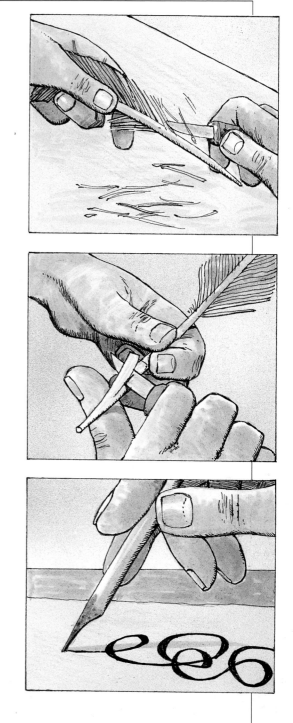

Writing lessons always took place in the boys' free time. In some towns, there were special writing schools, where the boys went in their holidays. There were also travelling writing teachers, who visited schools to give lessons. But some ushers also taught the skill. A writing lesson was an extra expense for parents. They had to pay the usher a teaching fee and provide paper, goose-feathers and ink. As a result, many poorer children learned to read without learning to write.

Children learned two styles of handwriting. Secretary was a flowing style, quick to write but difficult to read. Roman was a neater style with upright letters. It took longer to write so it was only used for important documents.

◀ Secretary script

▶ Roman handwriting

t is the part of a yonge man to reuerence his elders, and of suche, to choose out the beste and moste commended whose counsayle and auctoritie hee maye leane vnto: For the vnskilfulneße of tender yeares must by old mens experience, be ordered & gouern.

15

Difce puer
virtutem ex
me, verumque
laborem
Learn boy from
me virtue and
true labour
Virgil

AFTERNOON

▲ A monitor shows the boys how to recognize Roman numbers. Apart from that, very little maths was taught. The master often looked down on the subject, and most maths teaching was done by the usher.

Afternoon lessons began at one o'clock and carried on until five in winter, or six in summer. The lessons were much like those of the morning, with more Latin grammar and translation. It was a long day, and it must have been hard for the boys to concentrate by the end.

Tudor schools taught very little arithmetic. It was an extra subject, which the boys could learn in their spare time from the usher. Merchants and shopkeepers paid him an extra fee to teach their children how to keep accounts and do sums. The closest to arithmetic that most boys came was learning to recognize Roman numbers. This helped them find the numbered chapters and verses in the Bible.

▼ These boys are being tested on the Catechism – a set of questions and answers about the Christian religion. The master looks on to see how well they do. These lessons were often held on Saturday afternoons.

▲ On Sundays the boys had to go to church.

In the sixteenth century, wars were being fought all over Europe between the followers of two different sorts of Christianity. They were called Protestants and Catholics. England, once Catholic, had become a Protestant country, but many English people were still Catholic. One aim of Tudor teaching was to stamp out Catholic beliefs. The teachers wanted the boys to grow up to be good Protestants.

◄ Tudor education was nearly all about repeating and memorising facts and information. The most creative thing the boys did was to write imaginary letters on various subjects.

TIME OFF

The boys had time off on Sundays and on religious festivals, such as Christmas. These were called 'holy days', which is where our word 'holiday' comes from. There were also special half-days off, called 'remedies'. Remedies, often on a Thursday or Saturday afternoon, were given as a reward for good work.

▼ The boys are let out of school for a half-day holiday. They are making their way to a nearby field for a game of football. As they get out of sight of the master, their excitement gets the better of them!

◄ A game of football in Tudor times. Some schoolmasters tried to ban football, which was a much rougher game than it is now. There were no rules, and fighting often broke out. One writer, Sir Thomas Elyot, said that football was 'nothing but beastly fury and extreme violence.'

► A cockfight. Cockfighting was banned in some schools. It was not seen as cruel, but some masters thought it was a waste of time. Other masters enjoyed it as much as the boys.

Time off did not mean that the boys could do what they wanted. There was often homework to be done, and extra lessons, such as writing. On holy days, they were expected to go to church in the morning, marching two by two. At church, they all had to listen closely to the priest's sermon (speech). They were often tested about it on the following morning at school.

Despite everything, the boys always found time to play games. The younger boys played with hoops and spinning tops. In winter, all the boys skated on frozen ponds, or sledged in the snow. Football was a favourite game, played with a blown-up pig's bladder or a leather ball stuffed with hair. Another popular game was cockfighting. The boys stood in a circle and watched two cockerels fighting each other until one was too badly hurt to carry on.

THE SCHOOL PLAY

Many grammar schools put on a play at Christmas, often in Latin. The audience was made up of the boys' parents together with important local people. The play was seen as a good way of encouraging the boys to speak Latin. But it also gave the master the chance to show off his teaching.

Several types of play were performed. There were tragedies, plays showing the sufferings of a great hero or heroine; and comedies, light-hearted plays, often about love. These were mostly written by ancient Roman writers. Some masters wrote their own plays, in Latin or English. These might be based on a story from the Bible, or drawn from Roman history or myth.

▼ Actors performing for Queen Elizabeth Some London grammar schools were so good at putting on plays that they were asked to perform for the Queen. She loved watching plays, and she enjoyed the boys' shows as much as those put on by grown-up actors. This upset the actors and writers of London, who were losing work to the boys.

For the boys, the Christmas play meant more hard work. They had to learn their lines in their spare time. But it did make a welcome break from lessons.

◀ A stage play in a Tudor theatre.

▼ At Christmas, the boys put on a play set in ancient Rome. There were few costumes or props, just a couple of home-made wooden swords, a cloak and a standard. If the play included female parts, some of the boys had to dress as women.

THE END OF THE DAY

When the church bells rang out at five or six o'clock, the school day came to an end. A monitor collected the books and then all the boys knelt for more prayers, led by the master.

A teacher called Claudius Holleyband wrote a book in which he described a day in a Tudor school. At the end of the day, the master speaks to the boys: 'Rehearse after supper the lesson which you will learn tomorrow morning, and read it six or seven times. Then, having said your prayers, sleep on it. You shall see that tomorrow morning you will learn it easily. You shall be whipped tomorrow morning if you miss a word of it.'

▲ Gathering up books and putting them on the shelves.

▼ These boys are handing in the letters they wrote in the afternoon's lesson.

With this, the boys were set free. The day pupils went off to play games, or walked home. The boarders had bowls of pottage for supper, followed by an hour or two of free time. By eight o'clock, all the boys were in bed.

▼ Supper time for the boarders.

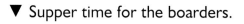

WHO DIDN'T GO TO SCHOOL?

GIRLS Girls could learn to read at petty school, but they got most of their education at home. Their mothers taught them to cook, sew, treat sickness and run a household. They learned about religion from their parents and by going to church.

RICH NOBLES Sons and daughters of the richest nobles were taught at home by private teachers called 'tutors'.

CATHOLICS English Catholics did not want to send their sons to grammar schools, which taught the Protestant religion. Their sons were taught at home by private Catholic tutors, often priests.

THE POOREST CHILDREN The sons of poor workers and farm labourers rarely went to grammar school. School fees could be cheap, but few poor people had any money to spare at all. It was more important for their sons to learn farming skills than to be able to write.

PLACES OF INTEREST

You can find out more about Britain in Tudor times by visiting some of these places:

1 Coughton Court, nr Alcester, Warwickshire (tel. 01789 762435). This Elizabethan house includes an exhibition on children's clothes.

2 Hampton Court Palace, Surrey KT8 9AU (tel. 0181 781 9500). The royal palace of Henry VIII.

3 Hardwick Hall, Chesterfield, Derbyshire S44 5QJ (tel. 01246 850430). A huge late sixteenth-century house with original Tudor furniture and tapestries.

4 Little Moreton Hall, Congleton, Cheshire CW12 4SD (tel. 01260 272018). A beautiful timber-framed manor house with a moat.

5 The Elizabethan House, 32 New Street, Plymouth PL1 2NA (tel. 01752 264878). A museum in an Elizabethan house that gives a good idea of everyday life.

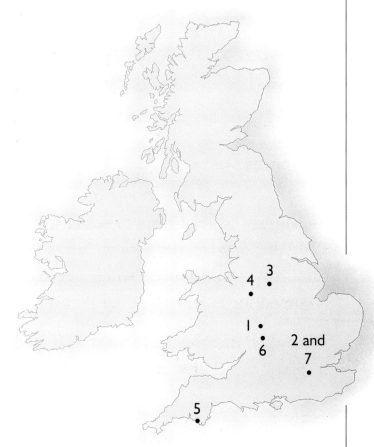

6 Shakespeare's Birthplace Museum, Henley Street, Stratford-upon-Avon CV37 6QW (tel. 01789 204016). The museum is in a house that was once owned by William Shakespeare's father.

7 Shakespeare's Globe Theatre, New Globe Walk, London SE1 (tel. 0171 928 6406). A reconstruction of Shakespeare's famous theatre, close to its original site. It includes an exhibition on the theatre, plays and actors in Tudor times.

INDEX

PICTURE ACKNOWLEDGEMENTS

ET Archive 19 right; Fotomas Index 8, 9, 11, 13; Hulton Getty 17, 20 right; Mary Evans Picture Library 19 top; RGC Library 5, 20 left. The map on page 23 is by Peter Bull.